CPSIA information can be obtained
at www.ICGtesting.com
Printed in the USA
LVHW022349070920
665258LV00017B/2080

9 781798 474600